Occupational Safety and Health Act of 1970

To assure safe and healthful working conditions
for working men and women; by authorizing
enforcement of the standards developed under
the Act; by assisting and encouraging the States in
their efforts to assure safe and healthful working
conditions; by providing for research, information,
education, and training in the field of occupational
safety and health; and for other purposes.

Public Law 91 596
84 STAT. 1590
91st Congress, S.2193
December 29, 1970,
as amended through January 1, 2004. [1]

An Act

To assure safe and healthful working conditions for working men and women; by authorizing enforcement of the standards developed under the Act; by assisting and encouraging the States in their efforts to assure safe and healthful working conditions; by providing for research, information, education, and training in the field of occupational safety and health; and for other purposes.

Be it enacted by the Senate and House of Representatives of the United States of America in Congress assembled, That this Act may be cited as the "Occupational Safety and Health Act of 1970."

SEC. 2. CONGRESSIONAL FINDINGS AND PURPOSE

(a) The Congress finds that personal injuries and illnesses arising out of work situations impose a substantial burden upon, and are a hindrance to, interstate commerce in terms of lost production, wage loss, medical expenses, and disability compensation payments.

29 USC 651

(b) The Congress declares it to be its purpose and policy, through the exercise of its powers to regulate commerce among the several States and with foreign nations and to provide for the general welfare, to assure so far as possible every working man and woman in the Nation safe and healthful working conditions and to preserve our human resources

(1) by encouraging employers and employees in their efforts to reduce the number of occupational safety and health hazards at their places of employ ment, and to stimulate employers and employees to institute new and to perfect existing programs for providing safe and healthful working conditions;

(2) by providing that employers and employees have separate but depen dent responsibilities and rights with respect to achieving safe and healthful working conditions;

(3) by authorizing the Secretary of Labor to set mandatory occupational safety and health standards applicable to businesses affecting interstate com merce, and by creating an Occupational Safety and Health Review Commission for carrying out adjudicatory functions under the Act;

(4) by building upon advances already made through employer and employee initiative for providing safe and healthful working conditions;

(5) by providing for research in the field of occupational safety and health, including the psychological factors involved, and by developing innovative methods, techniques, and approaches for dealing with occupational safety and health problems;

(6) by exploring ways to discover latent diseases, establishing causal con nections between diseases and work in environmental conditions, and con ducting other research relating to health problems, in recognition of the fact that occupational health standards present problems often different from those involved in occupational safety;

(7) by providing medical criteria which will assure insofar as practicable that no employee will suffer diminished health, functional capacity, or life expectancy as a result of his work experience;

(8) by providing for training programs to increase the number and compe tence of personnel engaged in the field of occupational safety and health;

Footnote [1] See Historical notes at the end of this document for changes and amendments affecting the OSH Act since its passage in 1970 through January 1, 2004.

29 USC 651

(9) by providing for the development and promulgation of occupational safety and health standards;

(10) by providing an effective enforcement program which shall include a prohibition against giving advance notice of any inspection and sanctions for any individual violating this prohibition;

(11) by encouraging the States to assume the fullest responsibility for the administration and enforcement of their occupational safety and health laws by providing grants to the States to assist in identifying their needs and responsibilities in the area of occupational safety and health, to develop plans in accordance with the provisions of this Act, to improve the administration and enforcement of State occupational safety and health laws, and to conduct experimental and demonstration projects in connection therewith;

(12) by providing for appropriate reporting procedures with respect to occupational safety and health which procedures will help achieve the objectives of this Act and accurately describe the nature of the occupational safety and health problem;

(13) by encouraging joint labor management efforts to reduce injuries and disease arising out of employment.

SEC. 3. DEFINITIONS

29 USC 652

For the purposes of this Act

(1) The term "Secretary" means the Secretary of Labor.

(2) The term "Commission" means the Occupational Safety and Health Review Commission established under this Act.

For Trust
Territory cover-
age, including the
Northern Mariana
Islands, *see
Historical notes.*

Pub. L. 105-241
United States
Postal Service is
an employer sub-
ject to the Act.
*See Historical
notes.*

(3) The term "commerce" means trade, traffic, commerce, transportation, or communication among the several States, or between a State and any place outside thereof, or within the District of Columbia, or a possession of the United States (other than the Trust Territory of the Pacific Islands), or between points in the same State but through a point outside thereof.

(4) The term "person" means one or more individuals, partnerships, associations, corporations, business trusts, legal representatives, or any organized group of persons.

(5) The term "employer" means a person engaged in a business affecting commerce who has employees, but does not include the United States (not including the United States Postal Service) or any State or political subdivision of a State.

(6) The term "employee" means an employee of an employer who is employed in a business of his employer which affects commerce.

(7) The term "State" includes a State of the United States, the District of Columbia, Puerto Rico, the Virgin Islands, American Samoa, Guam, and the Trust Territory of the Pacific Islands.

(8) The term "occupational safety and health standard" means a standard which requires conditions, or the adoption or use of one or more practices, means, methods, operations, or processes, reasonably necessary or appropriate to provide safe or healthful employment and places of employment.

(9) The term "national consensus standard" means any occupational safety and health standard or modification thereof which (1), has been adopted and promulgated by a nationally recognized standards producing organization under procedures whereby it can be determined by the Secretary that persons interested and affected by the scope or provisions of the standard have reached

29 USC 652

substantial agreement on its adoption, (2) was formulated in a manner which afforded an opportunity for diverse views to be considered and (3) has been designated as such a standard by the Secretary, after consultation with other appropriate Federal agencies.

(10) The term "established Federal standard" means any operative occupational safety and health standard established by any agency of the United States and presently in effect, or contained in any Act of Congress in force on the date of enactment of this Act.

(11) The term "Committee" means the National Advisory Committee on Occupational Safety and Health established under this Act.

(12) The term "Director" means the Director of the National Institute for Occupational Safety and Health.

(13) The term "Institute" means the National Institute for Occupational Safety and Health established under this Act.

(14) The term "Workmen's Compensation Commission" means the National Commission on State Workmen's Compensation Laws established under this Act.

SEC. 4. APPLICABILITY OF THIS ACT

(a) This Act shall apply with respect to employment performed in a workplace in a State, the District of Columbia, the Commonwealth of Puerto Rico, the Virgin Islands, American Samoa, Guam, the Trust Territory of the Pacific Islands, Wake Island, Outer Continental Shelf Lands defined in the Outer Continental Shelf Lands Act, Johnston Island, and the Canal Zone. The Secretary of the Interior shall, by regulation, provide for judicial enforcement of this Act by the courts established for areas in which there are no United States district courts having jurisdiction.

29 USC 653

For Canal Zone and Trust Territory coverage, including the Northern Mariana Islands, *see Historical notes.*

(b) (1) Nothing in this Act shall apply to working conditions of employees with respect to which other Federal agencies, and State agencies acting under section 274 of the Atomic Energy Act of 1954, as amended (42 U.S.C. 2021), exercise statutory authority to prescribe or enforce standards or regulations affecting occupational safety or health.

(2) The safety and health standards promulgated under the Act of June 30, 1936, commonly known as the Walsh Healey Act (41 U.S.C. 35 et seq.), the Service Contract Act of 1965 (41 U.S.C. 351 et seq.), Public Law 91 54, Act of August 9, 1969 (40 U.S.C. 333), Public Law 85 742, Act of August 23, 1958 (33 U.S.C. 941), and the National Foundation on Arts and Humanities Act (20 U.S.C. 951 et seq.) are superseded on the effective date of corresponding standards, promulgated under this Act, which are determined by the Secretary to be more effective. Standards issued under the laws listed in this paragraph and in effect on or after the effective date of this Act shall be deemed to be occupational safety and health standards issued under this Act, as well as under such other Acts.

(3) The Secretary shall, within three years after the effective date of this Act, report to the Congress his recommendations for legislation to avoid unnecessary duplication and to achieve coordination between this Act and other Federal laws.

(4) Nothing in this Act shall be construed to supersede or in any manner affect any workmen's compensation law or to enlarge or diminish or affect in any other manner the common law or statutory rights, duties, or liabilities of employers and employees under any law with respect to injuries, diseases, or death of employees arising out of, or in the course of, employment.

29 USC 654

SEC. 5. DUTIES

29 USC 654

(a) Each employer

(1) shall furnish to each of his employees employment and a place of employment which are free from recognized hazards that are causing or are likely to cause death or serious physical harm to his employees;

(2) shall comply with occupational safety and health standards promulgated under this Act.

(b) Each employee shall comply with occupational safety and health standards and all rules, regulations, and orders issued pursuant to this Act which are applicable to his own actions and conduct.

SEC. 6. OCCUPATIONAL SAFETY AND HEALTH STANDARDS

29 USC 655

(a) Without regard to chapter 5 of title 5, United States Code, or to the other subsections of this section, the Secretary shall, as soon as practicable during the period beginning with the effective date of this Act and ending two years after such date, by rule promulgate as an occupational safety or health standard any national consensus standard, and any established Federal standard, unless he determines that the promulgation of such a standard would not result in improved safety or health for specifically designated employees. In the event of conflict among any such standards, the Secretary shall promulgate the standard which assures the greatest protection of the safety or health of the affected employees.

(b) The Secretary may by rule promulgate, modify, or revoke any occupational safety or health standard in the following manner:

(1) Whenever the Secretary, upon the basis of information submitted to him in writing by an interested person, a representative of any organization of employers or employees, a nationally recognized standards producing organization, the Secretary of Health and Human Services, the National Institute for Occupational Safety and Health, or a State or political subdivision, or on the basis of information developed by the Secretary or otherwise available to him, determines that a rule should be promulgated in order to serve the objectives of this Act, the Secretary may request the recommendations of an advisory committee appointed under section 7 of this Act. The Secretary shall provide such an advisory committee with any proposals of his own or of the Secretary of Health and Human Services, together with all pertinent factual information developed by the Secretary or the Secretary of Health and Human Services, or otherwise available, including the results of research, demonstrations, and experiments. An advisory committee shall submit to the Secretary its recommendations regarding the rule to be promulgated within ninety days from the date of its appointment or within such longer or shorter period as may be prescribed by the Secretary, but in no event for a period which is longer than two hundred and seventy days.

(2) The Secretary shall publish a proposed rule promulgating, modifying, or revoking an occupational safety or health standard in the Federal Register and shall afford interested persons a period of thirty days after publication to submit written data or comments. Where an advisory committee is appointed and the Secretary determines that a rule should be issued, he shall publish the proposed rule within sixty days after the submission of the advisory committee's recommendations or the expiration of the period prescribed by the Secretary for such submission.

(3) On or before the last day of the period provided for the submission of written data or comments under paragraph (2), any interested person may file with the Secretary written objections to the proposed rule, stating the grounds

therefor and requesting a public hearing on such objections. Within thirty days after the last day for filing such objections, the Secretary shall publish in the Federal Register a notice specifying the occupational safety or health standard to which objections have been filed and a hearing requested, and specifying a time and place for such hearing.

(4) Within sixty days after the expiration of the period provided for the sub mission of written data or comments under paragraph (2), or within sixty days after the completion of any hearing held under paragraph (3), the Secretary shall issue a rule promulgating, modifying, or revoking an occupational safety or health standard or make a determination that a rule should not be issued. Such a rule may contain a provision delaying its effective date for such period (not in excess of ninety days) as the Secretary determines may be necessary to insure that affected employers and employees will be informed of the existence of the standard and of its terms and that employers affected are given an oppor tunity to familiarize themselves and their employees with the existence of the requirements of the standard.

(5) The Secretary, in promulgating standards dealing with toxic materials or harmful physical agents under this subsection, shall set the standard which most adequately assures, to the extent feasible, on the basis of the best avail able evidence, that no employee will suffer material impairment of health or functional capacity even if such employee has regular exposure to the hazard dealt with by such standard for the period of his working life. Development of standards under this subsection shall be based upon research, demonstrations, experiments, and such other information as may be appropriate. In addition to the attainment of the highest degree of health and safety protection for the employee, other considerations shall be the latest available scientific data in the field, the feasibility of the standards, and experience gained under this and other health and safety laws. Whenever practicable, the standard promulgated shall be expressed in terms of objective criteria and of the performance desired.

(6) (A) Any employer may apply to the Secretary for a temporary order granting a variance from a standard or any provision thereof promulgated under this section. Such temporary order shall be granted only if the employer files an application which meets the requirements of clause (B) and establish es that

(i) he is unable to comply with a standard by its effective date because of unavailability of professional or technical personnel or of materials and equipment needed to come into compliance with the standard or because necessary construction or alteration of facilities cannot be completed by the effective date,

(ii) he is taking all available steps to safeguard his employees against the hazards covered by the standard, and

(iii) he has an effective program for coming into compliance with the standard as quickly as practicable.

Any temporary order issued under this paragraph shall prescribe the practices, means, methods, operations, and processes which the employer must adopt and use while the order is in effect and state in detail his program for coming into compliance with the standard. Such a temporary order may be granted only after notice to employees and an opportunity for a hearing: *Provided,* That the Secretary may issue one interim order to be effective until a decision is made on the basis of the hearing. No temporary order may be in effect for longer than the period needed by the employer to achieve compliance with the standard or one year, whichever is shorter, except that such an order may be renewed not more that twice (I) so long as the requirements of this paragraph are met and (II) if an application for renewal is filed at least 90 days prior to the expiration date of the order. No interim renewal of an order may remain in effect for longer than 180 days.

(B) An application for temporary order under this paragraph (6) shall contain:

(i) a specification of the standard or portion thereof from which the employer seeks a variance,

(ii) a representation by the employer, supported by representations from qualified persons having firsthand knowledge of the facts represented, that he is unable to comply with the standard or portion thereof and a detailed statement of the reasons therefor,

(iii) a statement of the steps he has taken and will take (with specific dates) to protect employees against the hazard covered by the standard,

(iv) a statement of when he expects to be able to comply with the stan dard and what steps he has taken and what steps he will take (with dates specified) to come into compliance with the standard, and

(v) a certification that he has informed his employees of the application by giving a copy thereof to their authorized representative, posting a state ment giving a summary of the application and specifying where a copy may be examined at the place or places where notices to employees are normally posted, and by other appropriate means.

A description of how employees have been informed shall be con tained in the certification. The information to employees shall also inform them of their right to petition the Secretary for a hearing.

(C) The Secretary is authorized to grant a variance from any standard or portion thereof whenever he determines, or the Secretary of Health and Human Services certifies, that such variance is necessary to permit an employer to participate in an experiment approved by him or the Secretary of Health and Human Services designed to demonstrate or validate new and improved techniques to safeguard the health or safety of workers.

(7) Any standard promulgated under this subsection shall prescribe the use of labels or other appropriate forms of warning as are necessary to insure that employees are apprised of all hazards to which they are exposed, relevant symptoms and appropriate emergency treatment, and proper conditions and precautions of safe use or exposure. Where appropriate, such standard shall also prescribe suitable protective equipment and control or technological pro cedures to be used in connection with such hazards and shall provide for mon itoring or measuring employee exposure at such locations and intervals, and in such manner as may be necessary for the protection of employees. In addition, where appropriate, any such standard shall prescribe the type and frequency of medical examinations or other tests which shall be made available, by the employer or at his cost, to employees exposed to such hazards in order to most effectively determine whether the health of such employees is adversely affect ed by such exposure. In the event such medical examinations are in the nature of research, as determined by the Secretary of Health and Human Services, such examinations may be furnished at the expense of the Secretary of Health and Human Services. The results of such examinations or tests shall be fur nished only to the Secretary or the Secretary of Health and Human Services, and, at the request of the employee, to his physician. The Secretary, in consul tation with the Secretary of Health and Human Services, may by rule promul gated pursuant to section 553 of title 5, United States Code, make appropriate modifications in the foregoing requirements relating to the use of labels or other forms of warning, monitoring or measuring, and medical examinations, as may be warranted by experience, information, or medical or technological developments acquired subsequent to the promulgation of the relevant standard.

29 USC 655

(8) Whenever a rule promulgated by the Secretary differs substantially from an existing national consensus standard, the Secretary shall, at the same time, publish in the Federal Register a statement of the reasons why the rule as adopted will better effectuate the purposes of this Act than the national con sensus standard.

(c) (1) The Secretary shall provide, without regard to the requirements of chap ter 5, title 5, Unites States Code, for an emergency temporary standard to take immediate effect upon publication in the Federal Register if he determines

(A) that employees are exposed to grave danger from exposure to sub stances or agents determined to be toxic or physically harmful or from new hazards, and

(B) that such emergency standard is necessary to protect employees from such danger.

(2) Such standard shall be effective until superseded by a standard prom ulgated in accordance with the procedures prescribed in paragraph (3) of this subsection.

(3) Upon publication of such standard in the Federal Register the Secretary shall commence a proceeding in accordance with section 6 (b) of this Act, and the standard as published shall also serve as a proposed rule for the proceed ing. The Secretary shall promulgate a standard under this paragraph no later than six months after publication of the emergency standard as provided in paragraph (2) of this subsection.

(d) Any affected employer may apply to the Secretary for a rule or order for a variance from a standard promulgated under this section. Affected employees shall be given notice of each such application and an opportunity to participate in a hear ing. The Secretary shall issue such rule or order if he determines on the record, after opportunity for an inspection where appropriate and a hearing, that the proponent of the variance has demonstrated by a preponderance of the evidence that the con ditions, practices, means, methods, operations, or processes used or proposed to be used by an employer will provide employment and places of employment to his employees which are as safe and healthful as those which would prevail if he com plied with the standard. The rule or order so issued shall prescribe the conditions the employer must maintain, and the practices, means, methods, operations, and processes which he must adopt and utilize to the extent they differ from the stan dard in question. Such a rule or order may be modified or revoked upon applica tion by an employer, employees, or by the Secretary on his own motion, in the manner prescribed for its issuance under this subsection at any time after six months from its issuance.

(e) Whenever the Secretary promulgates any standard, makes any rule, order, or decision, grants any exemption or extension of time, or compromises, mitigates, or settles any penalty assessed under this Act, he shall include a statement of the reasons for such action, which shall be published in the Federal Register.

(f) Any person who may be adversely affected by a standard issued under this section may at any time prior to the sixtieth day after such standard is promulgat ed file a petition challenging the validity of such standard with the United States court of appeals for the circuit wherein such person resides or has his principal place of business, for a judicial review of such standard. A copy of the petition shall be forthwith transmitted by the clerk of the court to the Secretary. The filing of such petition shall not, unless otherwise ordered by the court, operate as a stay of the standard. The determinations of the Secretary shall be conclusive if supported by substantial evidence in the record considered as a whole.

(g) In determining the priority for establishing standards under this section, the Secretary shall give due regard to the urgency of the need for mandatory safety and health standards for particular industries, trades, crafts, occupations, businesses,

29 USC 655

workplaces or work environments. The Secretary shall also give due regard to the recommendations of the Secretary of Health and Human Services regarding the need for mandatory standards in determining the priority for establishing such stan dards.

SEC. 7. ADVISORY COMMITTEES; ADMINISTRATION

29 USC 656

(a) (1) There is hereby established a National Advisory Committee on Occupational Safety and Health consisting of twelve members appointed by the Secretary, four of whom are to be designated by the Secretary of Health and Human Services, without regard to the provisions of title 5, United States Code, governing appointments in the competitive service, and composed of representatives of management, labor, occupational safety and occupational health professions, and of the public. The Secretary shall designate one of the public members as Chairman. The members shall be selected upon the basis of their experience and competence in the field of occupational safety and health.

(2) The Committee shall advise, consult with, and make recommendations to the Secretary and the Secretary of Health and Human Services on matters relating to the administration of the Act. The Committee shall hold no fewer than two meetings during each calendar year. All meetings of the Committee shall be open to the public and a transcript shall be kept and made available for public inspection.

(3) The members of the Committee shall be compensated in accordance with the provisions of section 3109 of title 5, United States Code.

(4) The Secretary shall furnish to the Committee an executive secretary and such secretarial, clerical, and other services as are deemed necessary to the con duct of its business.

(b) An advisory committee may be appointed by the Secretary to assist him in his standard setting functions under section 6 of this Act. Each such committee shall consist of not more than fifteen members and shall include as a member one or more designees of the Secretary of Health and Human Services, and shall include among its members an equal number of persons qualified by experience and affiliation to present the viewpoint of the employers involved, and of persons similarly qualified to present the viewpoint of the workers involved, as well as one or more representatives of health and safety agencies of the States. An advisory committee may also include such other persons as the Secretary may appoint who are qualified by knowledge and experience to make a useful contribution to the work of such committee, including one or more representatives of professional organizations of technicians or professionals specializing in occupational safety or health, and one or more representatives of nationally recognized standards producing organizations, but the number of persons so appointed to any such advi sory committee shall not exceed the number appointed to such committee as rep resentatives of Federal and State agencies. Persons appointed to advisory commit tees from private life shall be compensated in the same manner as consultants or experts under section 3109 of title 5, United States Code. The Secretary shall pay to any State which is the employer of a member of such a committee who is a rep resentative of the health or safety agency of that State, reimbursement sufficient to cover the actual cost to the State resulting from such representative's membership on such committee. Any meeting of such committee shall be open to the public and an accurate record shall be kept and made available to the public. No member of such committee (other than representatives of employers and employees) shall have an economic interest in any proposed rule.

(c) In carrying out his responsibilities under this Act, the Secretary is author ized to

(1) use, with the consent of any Federal agency, the services, facilities, and personnel of such agency, with or without reimbursement, and with the consent of any State or political subdivision thereof, accept and use the services, facil ities, and personnel of any agency of such State or subdivision with reim bursement; and

(2) employ experts and consultants or organizations thereof as authorized by section 3109 of title 5, United States Code, except that contracts for such employment may be renewed annually; compensate individuals so employed at rates not in excess of the rate specified at the time of service for grade GS 18 under section 5332 of title 5, United States Code, including travel time, and allow them while away from their homes or regular places of business, travel expenses (including per diem in lieu of subsistence) as authorized by section 5703 of title 5, United States Code, for persons in the Government service employed intermittently, while so employed.

SEC. 8. INSPECTIONS, INVESTIGATIONS, AND RECORDKEEPING

(a) In order to carry out the purposes of this Act, the Secretary, upon presenting appropriate credentials to the owner, operator, or agent in charge, is authorized

29 USC 657

(1) to enter without delay and at reasonable times any factory, plant, estab lishment, construction site, or other area, workplace or environment where work is performed by an employee of an employer; and

(2) to inspect and investigate during regular working hours and at other rea sonable times, and within reasonable limits and in a reasonable manner, any such place of employment and all pertinent conditions, structures, machines, apparatus, devices, equipment, and materials therein, and to question privately any such employer, owner, operator, agent or employee.

(b) In making his inspections and investigations under this Act the Secretary may require the attendance and testimony of witnesses and the production of evi dence under oath. Witnesses shall be paid the same fees and mileage that are paid witnesses in the courts of the United States. In case of a contumacy, failure, or refusal of any person to obey such an order, any district court of the United States or the United States courts of any territory or possession, within the jurisdiction of which such person is found, or resides or transacts business, upon the application by the Secretary, shall have jurisdiction to issue to such person an order requiring such person to appear to produce evidence if, as, and when so ordered, and to give testi mony relating to the matter under investigation or in question, and any failure to obey such order of the court may be punished by said court as a contempt thereof.

(c) (1) Each employer shall make, keep and preserve, and make available to the Secretary or the Secretary of Health and Human Services, such records regard ing his activities relating to this Act as the Secretary, in cooperation with the Secretary of Health and Human Services, may prescribe by regulation as nec essary or appropriate for the enforcement of this Act or for developing infor mation regarding the causes and prevention of occupational accidents and ill nesses. In order to carry out the provisions of this paragraph such regulations may include provisions requiring employers to conduct periodic inspections. The Secretary shall also issue regulations requiring that employers, through posting of notices or other appropriate means, keep their employees informed of their protections and obligations under this Act, including the provisions of applicable standards.

(2) The Secretary, in cooperation with the Secretary of Health and Human Services, shall prescribe regulations requiring employers to maintain accurate

records of, and to make periodic reports on, work related deaths, injuries and illnesses other than minor injuries requiring only first aid treatment and which do not involve medical treatment, loss of consciousness, restriction of work or motion, or transfer to another job.

(3) The Secretary, in cooperation with the Secretary of Health and Human Services, shall issue regulations requiring employers to maintain accurate records of employee exposures to potentially toxic materials or harmful phys ical agents which are required to be monitored or measured under section 6. Such regulations shall provide employees or their representatives with an opportunity to observe such monitoring or measuring, and to have access to the records thereof. Such regulations shall also make appropriate provision for each employee or former employee to have access to such records as will indi cate his own exposure to toxic materials or harmful physical agents. Each employer shall promptly notify any employee who has been or is being exposed to toxic materials or harmful physical agents in concentrations or at levels which exceed those prescribed by an applicable occupational safety and health standard promulgated under section 6, and shall inform any employee who is being thus exposed of the corrective action being taken.

(d) Any information obtained by the Secretary, the Secretary of Health and Human Services, or a State agency under this Act shall be obtained with a mini mum burden upon employers, especially those operating small businesses. Unnecessary duplication of efforts in obtaining information shall be reduced to the maximum extent feasible.

(e) Subject to regulations issued by the Secretary, a representative of the employer and a representative authorized by his employees shall be given an opportunity to accompany the Secretary or his authorized representative during the physical inspection of any workplace under subsection (a) for the purpose of aid ing such inspection. Where there is no authorized employee representative, the Secretary or his authorized representative shall consult with a reasonable number of employees concerning matters of health and safety in the workplace.

(f) (1) Any employees or representative of employees who believe that a vio lation of a safety or health standard exists that threatens physical harm, or that an imminent danger exists, may request an inspection by giving notice to the Secretary or his authorized representative of such violation or danger. Any such notice shall be reduced to writing, shall set forth with reasonable particularity the grounds for the notice, and shall be signed by the employees or representa tive of employees, and a copy shall be provided the employer or his agent no later than at the time of inspection, except that, upon the request of the person giving such notice, his name and the names of individual employees referred to therein shall not appear in such copy or on any record published, released, or made available pursuant to subsection (g) of this section. If upon receipt of such notification the Secretary determines there are reasonable grounds to believe that such violation or danger exists, he shall make a special inspection in accordance with the provisions of this section as soon as practicable, to determine if such violation or danger exists. If the Secretary determines there are no reasonable grounds to believe that a violation or danger exists he shall notify the employees or representative of the employees in writing of such determination.

(2) Prior to or during any inspection of a workplace, any employees or rep resentative of employees employed in such workplace may notify the Secretary or any representative of the Secretary responsible for conducting the inspec tion, in writing, of any violation of this Act which they have reason to believe exists in such workplace. The Secretary shall, by regulation, establish proce dures for informal review of any refusal by a representative of the Secretary to

29 USC 657

issue a citation with respect to any such alleged violation and shall furnish the employees or representative of employees requesting such review a written statement of the reasons for the Secretary's final disposition of the case.

(g) (1) The Secretary and Secretary of Health and Human Services are author ized to compile, analyze, and publish, either in summary or detailed form, all reports or information obtained under this section.

(2) The Secretary and the Secretary of Health and Human Services shall each prescribe such rules and regulations as he may deem necessary to carry out their responsibilities under this Act, including rules and regulations dealing with the inspection of an employer's establishment.

(h) The Secretary shall not use the results of enforcement activities, such as the number of citations issued or penalties assessed, to evaluate employees directly involved in enforcement activities under this Act or to impose quotas or goals with regard to the results of such activities.

Pub. L. 105-198 added subsection (h).

SEC. 9. CITATIONS

(a) If, upon inspection or investigation, the Secretary or his authorized repre sentative believes that an employer has violated a requirement of section 5 of this Act, of any standard, rule or order promulgated pursuant to section 6 of this Act, or of any regulations prescribed pursuant to this Act, he shall with reasonable prompt ness issue a citation to the employer. Each citation shall be in writing and shall describe with particularity the nature of the violation, including a reference to the provision of the Act, standard, rule, regulation, or order alleged to have been vio lated. In addition, the citation shall fix a reasonable time for the abatement of the violation. The Secretary may prescribe procedures for the issuance of a notice in lieu of a citation with respect to de minimis violations which have no direct or immediate relationship to safety or health.

29 USC 658

(b) Each citation issued under this section, or a copy or copies thereof, shall be prominently posted, as prescribed in regulations issued by the Secretary, at or near each place a violation referred to in the citation occurred.

(c) No citation may be issued under this section after the expiration of six months following the occurrence of any violation.

SEC. 10. PROCEDURE FOR ENFORCEMENT

(a) If, after an inspection or investigation, the Secretary issues a citation under section 9(a), he shall, within a reasonable time after the termination of such inspec tion or investigation, notify the employer by certified mail of the penalty, if any, proposed to be assessed under section 17 and that the employer has fifteen work ing days within which to notify the Secretary that he wishes to contest the citation or proposed assessment of penalty. If, within fifteen working days from the receipt of the notice issued by the Secretary the employer fails to notify the Secretary that he intends to contest the citation or proposed assessment of penalty, and no notice is filed by any employee or representative of employees under subsection (c) within such time, the citation and the assessment, as proposed, shall be deemed a final order of the Commission and not subject to review by any court or agency.

29 USC 659

(b) If the Secretary has reason to believe that an employer has failed to correct a violation for which a citation has been issued within the period permitted for its correction (which period shall not begin to run until the entry of a final order by the Commission in the case of any review proceedings under this section initiated by the employer in good faith and not solely for delay or avoidance of penalties), the Secretary shall notify the employer by certified mail of such failure and of the penalty proposed to be assessed under section 17 by reason of such failure, and that

29 USC 659

the employer has fifteen working days within which to notify the Secretary that he wishes to contest the Secretary's notification or the proposed assessment of penalty. If, within fifteen working days from the receipt of notification issued by the Secretary, the employer fails to notify the Secretary that he intends to contest the notification or proposed assessment of penalty, the notification and assessment, as proposed, shall be deemed a final order of the Commission and not subject to review by any court or agency.

(c) If an employer notifies the Secretary that he intends to contest a citation issued under section 9(a) or notification issued under subsection (a) or (b) of this section, or if, within fifteen working days of the issuance of a citation under sec tion 9(a), any employee or representative of employees files a notice with the Secretary alleging that the period of time fixed in the citation for the abatement of the violation is unreasonable, the Secretary shall immediately advise the Commission of such notification, and the Commission shall afford an opportunity for a hearing (in accordance with section 554 of title 5, United States Code, but without regard to subsection (a)(3) of such section). The Commission shall there after issue an order, based on findings of fact, affirming, modifying, or vacating the Secretary's citation or proposed penalty, or directing other appropriate relief, and such order shall become final thirty days after its issuance. Upon a showing by an employer of a good faith effort to comply with the abatement requirements of a citation, and that abatement has not been completed because of factors beyond his reasonable control, the Secretary, after an opportunity for a hearing as provided in this subsection, shall issue an order affirming or modifying the abatement require ments in such citation. The rules of procedure prescribed by the Commission shall provide affected employees or representatives of affected employees an opportu nity to participate as parties to hearings under this subsection.

SEC. 11. JUDICIAL REVIEW

29 USC 660

(a) Any person adversely affected or aggrieved by an order of the Commission issued under subsection (c) of section 10 may obtain a review of such order in any United States court of appeals for the circuit in which the violation is alleged to have occurred or where the employer has its principal office, or in the Court of Appeals for the District of Columbia Circuit, by filing in such court within sixty days following the issuance of such order a written petition praying that the order be modified or set aside. A copy of such petition shall be forthwith transmitted by the clerk of the court to the Commission and to the other parties, and thereupon the Commission shall file in the court the record in the proceeding as provided in sec tion 2112 of title 28, United States Code. Upon such filing, the court shall have jurisdiction of the proceeding and of the question determined therein, and shall have power to grant such temporary relief or restraining order as it deems just and proper, and to make and enter upon the pleadings, testimony, and proceedings set forth in such record a decree affirming, modifying, or setting aside in whole or in part, the order of the Commission and enforcing the same to the extent that such order is affirmed or modified. The commencement of proceedings under this sub section shall not, unless ordered by the court, operate as a stay of the order of the Commission. No objection that has not been urged before the Commission shall be considered by the court, unless the failure or neglect to urge such objection shall be excused because of extraordinary circumstances. The findings of the Commission with respect to questions of fact, if supported by substantial evidence on the record considered as a whole, shall be conclusive. If any party shall apply to the court for leave to adduce additional evidence and shall show to the satisfac tion of the court that such additional evidence is material and that there were rea

29 USC 660

sonable grounds for the failure to adduce such evidence in the hearing before the Commission, the court may order such additional evidence to be taken before the Commission and to be made a part of the record. The Commission may modify its findings as to the facts, or make new findings, by reason of additional evidence so taken and filed, and it shall file such modified or new findings, which findings with respect to questions of fact, if supported by substantial evidence on the record con sidered as a whole, shall be conclusive, and its recommendations, if any, for the modification or setting aside of its original order. Upon the filing of the record with it, the jurisdiction of the court shall be exclusive and its judgment and decree shall be final, except that the same shall be subject to review by the Supreme Court of the United States, as provided in section 1254 of title 28, United States Code.

Pub. L. 98-620

(b) The Secretary may also obtain review or enforcement of any final order of the Commission by filing a petition for such relief in the United States court of appeals for the circuit in which the alleged violation occurred or in which the employer has its principal office, and the provisions of subsection (a) shall govern such proceedings to the extent applicable. If no petition for review, as provided in subsection (a), is filed within sixty days after service of the Commission's order, the Commission's findings of fact and order shall be conclusive in connection with any petition for enforcement which is filed by the Secretary after the expiration of such sixty day period. In any such case, as well as in the case of a noncontested citation or notification by the Secretary which has become a final order of the Commission under subsection (a) or (b) of section 10, the clerk of the court, unless otherwise ordered by the court, shall forthwith enter a decree enforcing the order and shall transmit a copy of such decree to the Secretary and the employer named in the petition. In any contempt proceeding brought to enforce a decree of a court of appeals entered pursuant to this subsection or subsection (a), the court of appeals may assess the penalties provided in section 17, in addition to invoking any other available remedies.

(c) (1) No person shall discharge or in any manner discriminate against any employee because such employee has filed any complaint or instituted or caused to be instituted any proceeding under or related to this Act or has testi fied or is about to testify in any such proceeding or because of the exercise by such employee on behalf of himself or others of any right afforded by this Act.

(2) Any employee who believes that he has been discharged or otherwise discriminated against by any person in violation of this subsection may, with in thirty days after such violation occurs, file a complaint with the Secretary alleging such discrimination. Upon receipt of such complaint, the Secretary shall cause such investigation to be made as he deems appropriate. If upon such investigation, the Secretary determines that the provisions of this subsection have been violated, he shall bring an action in any appropriate United States district court against such person. In any such action the United States district courts shall have jurisdiction, for cause shown to restrain violations of para graph (1) of this subsection and order all appropriate relief including rehiring or reinstatement of the employee to his former position with back pay.

(3) Within 90 days of the receipt of a complaint filed under this subsection the Secretary shall notify the complainant of his determination under paragraph 2 of this subsection.

SEC. 12. THE OCCUPATIONAL SAFETY AND HEALTH REVIEW COMMISSION

(a) The Occupational Safety and Health Review Commission is hereby estab lished. The Commission shall be composed of three members who shall be appointed by the President, by and with the advice and consent of the Senate, from

29 USC 661

29 USC 661

among persons who by reason of training, education, or experience are qualified to carry out the functions of the Commission under this Act. The President shall des ignate one of the members of the Commission to serve as Chairman.

(b) The terms of members of the Commission shall be six years except that

(1) the members of the Commission first taking office shall serve, as designat ed by the President at the time of appointment, one for a term of two years, one for a term of four years, and one for a term of six years, and

(2) a vacancy caused by the death, resignation, or removal of a member prior to the expiration of the term for which he was appointed shall be filled only for the remainder of such unexpired term.

A member of the Commission may be removed by the President for inefficiency, neglect of duty, or malfeasance in office.

See notes on omitted text.

(c) (Text omitted.)

(d) The principal office of the Commission shall be in the District of Columbia. Whenever the Commission deems that the convenience of the public or of the par ties may be promoted, or delay or expense may be minimized, it may hold hear ings or conduct other proceedings at any other place.

Pub. L. 95-251

(e) The Chairman shall be responsible on behalf of the Commission for the administrative operations of the Commission and shall appoint such administrative law judges and other employees as he deems necessary to assist in the performance of the Commission's functions and to fix their compensation in accordance with the provisions of chapter 51 and subchapter III of chapter 53 of title 5, United States Code, relating to classification and General Schedule pay rates: *Provided,* That assignment, removal and compensation of administrative law judges shall be in accordance with sections 3105, 3344, 5372, and 7521 of title 5, United States Code.

(f) For the purpose of carrying out its functions under this Act, two members of the Commission shall constitute a quorum and official action can be taken only on the affirmative vote of at least two members.

(g) Every official act of the Commission shall be entered of record, and its hear ings and records shall be open to the public. The Commission is authorized to make such rules as are necessary for the orderly transaction of its proceedings. Unless the Commission has adopted a different rule, its proceedings shall be in accordance with the Federal Rules of Civil Procedure.

(h) The Commission may order testimony to be taken by deposition in any pro ceedings pending before it at any state of such proceeding. Any person may be compelled to appear and depose, and to produce books, papers, or documents, in the same manner as witnesses may be compelled to appear and testify and produce like documentary evidence before the Commission. Witnesses whose depositions are taken under this subsection, and the persons taking such depositions, shall be entitled to the same fees as are paid for like services in the courts of the United States.

(i) For the purpose of any proceeding before the Commission, the provisions of section 11 of the National Labor Relations Act (29 U.S.C. 161) are hereby made applicable to the jurisdiction and powers of the Commission.

(j) An administrative law judge appointed by the Commission shall hear, and make a determination upon, any proceeding instituted before the Commission and any motion in connection therewith, assigned to such administrative law judge by the Chairman of the Commission, and shall make a report of any such determina tion which constitutes his final disposition of the proceedings. The report of the administrative law judge shall become the final order of the Commission within

29 USC 661

thirty days after such report by the administrative law judge, unless within such period any Commission member has directed that such report shall be reviewed by the Commission.

(k) Except as otherwise provided in this Act, the administrative law judges shall be subject to the laws governing employees in the classified civil service, except that appointments shall be made without regard to section 5108 of title 5, United States Code. Each administrative law judge shall receive compensation at a rate not less than that prescribed for GS 16 under section 5332 of title 5, United States Code.

SEC. 13. PROCEDURES TO COUNTERACT IMMINENT DANGERS

29 USC 662

(a) The United States district courts shall have jurisdiction, upon petition of the Secretary, to restrain any conditions or practices in any place of employment which are such that a danger exists which could reasonably be expected to cause death or serious physical harm immediately or before the imminence of such danger can be eliminated through the enforcement procedures otherwise provided by this Act. Any order issued under this section may require such steps to be taken as may be necessary to avoid, correct, or remove such imminent danger and prohibit the employment or presence of any individual in locations or under conditions where such imminent danger exists, except individuals whose presence is necessary to avoid, correct, or remove such imminent danger or to maintain the capacity of a continuous process operation to resume normal operations without a complete ces sation of operations, or where a cessation of operations is necessary, to permit such to be accomplished in a safe and orderly manner.

(b) Upon the filing of any such petition the district court shall have jurisdiction to grant such injunctive relief or temporary restraining order pending the outcome of an enforcement proceeding pursuant to this Act. The proceeding shall be as pro vided by Rule 65 of the Federal Rules, Civil Procedure, except that no temporary restraining order issued without notice shall be effective for a period longer than five days.

(c) Whenever and as soon as an inspector concludes that conditions or practices described in subsection (a) exist in any place of employment, he shall inform the affected employees and employers of the danger and that he is recommending to the Secretary that relief be sought.

(d) If the Secretary arbitrarily or capriciously fails to seek relief under this sec tion, any employee who may be injured by reason of such failure, or the represen tative of such employees, might bring an action against the Secretary in the United States district court for the district in which the imminent danger is alleged to exist or the employer has its principal office, or for the District of Columbia, for a writ of mandamus to compel the Secretary to seek such an order and for such further relief as may be appropriate.

SEC. 14. REPRESENTATION IN CIVIL LITIGATION

29 USC 663

Except as provided in section 518(a) of title 28, United States Code, relating to litigation before the Supreme Court, the Solicitor of Labor may appear for and represent the Secretary in any civil litigation brought under this Act but all such litigation shall be subject to the direction and control of the Attorney General.

29 USC 664

SEC. 15. CONFIDENTIALITY OF TRADE SECRETS

29 USC 664

All information reported to or otherwise obtained by the Secretary or his rep resentative in connection with any inspection or proceeding under this Act which contains or which might reveal a trade secret referred to in section 1905 of title 18 of the United States Code shall be considered confidential for the purpose of that section, except that such information may be disclosed to other officers or employ ees concerned with carrying out this Act or when relevant in any proceeding under this Act. In any such proceeding the Secretary, the Commission, or the court shall issue such orders as may be appropriate to protect the confidentiality of trade secrets.

SEC. 16. VARIATIONS, TOLERANCES, AND EXEMPTIONS

29 USC 665

The Secretary, on the record, after notice and opportunity for a hearing may provide such reasonable limitations and may make such rules and regulations allowing reasonable variations, tolerances, and exemptions to and from any or all provisions of this Act as he may find necessary and proper to avoid serious impair ment of the national defense. Such action shall not be in effect for more than six months without notification to affected employees and an opportunity being afforded for a hearing.

SEC. 17. PENALTIES

29 USC 666

Pub. L. 101-508 increased the civil penalties in sub- sections (a)-(d) & (i). *See Historical notes.*

(a) Any employer who willfully or repeatedly violates the requirements of sec tion 5 of this Act, any standard, rule, or order promulgated pursuant to section 6 of this Act, or regulations prescribed pursuant to this Act, may be assessed a civil penalty of not more than $70,000 for each violation, but not less than $5,000 for each willful violation.

(b) Any employer who has received a citation for a serious violation of the requirements of section 5 of this Act, of any standard, rule, or order promulgated pursuant to section 6 of this Act, or of any regulations prescribed pursuant to this Act, shall be assessed a civil penalty of up to $7,000 for each such violation.

(c) Any employer who has received a citation for a violation of the require ments of section 5 of this Act, of any standard, rule, or order promulgated pursuant to section 6 of this Act, or of regulations prescribed pursuant to this Act, and such violation is specifically determined not to be of a serious nature, may be assessed a civil penalty of up to $7,000 for each violation.

(d) Any employer who fails to correct a violation for which a citation has been issued under section 9(a) within the period permitted for its correction (which peri od shall not begin to run until the date of the final order of the Commission in the case of any review proceeding under section 10 initiated by the employer in good faith and not solely for delay or avoidance of penalties), may be assessed a civil penalty of not more than $7,000 for each day during which such failure or viola tion continues.

Pub. L. 98-473 Maximum criminal fines are increased by the Sentencing Reform Act of 1984, 18 USC § 3551 et seq. *See Historical notes.*

(e) Any employer who willfully violates any standard, rule, or order promul gated pursuant to section 6 of this Act, or of any regulations prescribed pursuant to this Act, and that violation caused death to any employee, shall, upon conviction, be punished by a fine of not more than $10,000 or by imprisonment for not more than six months, or by both; except that if the conviction is for a violation com mitted after a first conviction of such person, punishment shall be by a fine of not more than $20,000 or by imprisonment for not more than one year, or by both.

(f) Any person who gives advance notice of any inspection to be conducted under this Act, without authority from the Secretary or his designees, shall, upon conviction, be punished by a fine of not more than $1,000 or by imprisonment for not more than six months, or by both.

29 USC 666

(g) Whoever knowingly makes any false statement, representation, or certifi cation in any application, record, report, plan, or other document filed or required to be maintained pursuant to this Act shall, upon conviction, be punished by a fine of not more than $10,000, or by imprisonment for not more than six months, or by both.

(h) (1) Section 1114 of title 18, United States Code, is hereby amended by strik ing out "designated by the Secretary of Health and Human Services to conduct investigations, or inspections under the Federal Food, Drug, and Cosmetic Act" and inserting in lieu thereof "or of the Department of Labor assigned to per form investigative, inspection, or law enforcement functions". *See historical notes.*

(2) Notwithstanding the provisions of sections 1111 and 1114 of title 18, United States Code, whoever, in violation of the provisions of section 1114 of such title, kills a person while engaged in or on account of the performance of investigative, inspection, or law enforcement functions added to such section 1114 by paragraph (1) of this subsection, and who would otherwise be subject to the penalty provisions of such section 1111, shall be punished by imprison ment for any term of years or for life.

(i) Any employer who violates any of the posting requirements, as prescribed under the provisions of this Act, shall be assessed a civil penalty of up to $7,000 for each violation.

(j) The Commission shall have authority to assess all civil penalties provided in this section, giving due consideration to the appropriateness of the penalty with respect to the size of the business of the employer being charged, the gravity of the violation, the good faith of the employer, and the history of previous violations.

(k) For purposes of this section, a serious violation shall be deemed to exist in a place of employment if there is a substantial probability that death or serious physical harm could result from a condition which exists, or from one or more practices, means, methods, operations, or processes which have been adopted or are in use, in such place of employment unless the employer did not, and could not with the exercise of reasonable diligence, know of the presence of the violation.

(l) Civil penalties owed under this Act shall be paid to the Secretary for deposit into the Treasury of the United States and shall accrue to the United States and may be recovered in a civil action in the name of the United States brought in the United States district court for the district where the violation is alleged to have occurred or where the employer has its principal office.

SEC. 18. STATE JURISDICTION AND STATE PLANS

(a) Nothing in this Act shall prevent any State agency or court from asserting jurisdiction under State law over any occupational safety or health issue with respect to which no standard is in effect under section 6. 29 USC 667

(b) Any State which, at any time, desires to assume responsibility for develop ment and enforcement therein of occupational safety and health standards relating to any occupational safety or health issue with respect to which a Federal standard has been promulgated under section 6 shall submit a State plan for the development of such standards and their enforcement.

(c) The Secretary shall approve the plan submitted by a State under subsection (b), or any modification thereof, if such plan in his judgement

(1) designates a State agency or agencies as the agency or agencies respon sible for administering the plan throughout the State,

(2) provides for the development and enforcement of safety and health standards relating to one or more safety or health issues, which standards (and the enforcement of which standards) are or will be at least as effective in pro viding safe and healthful employment and places of employment as the stan dards promulgated under section 6 which relate to the same issues, and which

standards, when applicable to products which are distributed or used in inter state commerce, are required by compelling local conditions and do not undu ly burden interstate commerce,

(3) provides for a right of entry and inspection of all workplaces subject to the Act which is at least as effective as that provided in section 8, and includes a prohibition on advance notice of inspections,

(4) contains satisfactory assurances that such agency or agencies have or will have the legal authority and qualified personnel necessary for the enforce ment of such standards,

(5) gives satisfactory assurances that such State will devote adequate funds to the administration and enforcement of such standards,

(6) contains satisfactory assurances that such State will, to the extent per mitted by its law, establish and maintain an effective and comprehensive occu pational safety and health program applicable to all employees of public agen cies of the State and its political subdivisions, which program is as effective as the standards contained in an approved plan,

(7) requires employers in the State to make reports to the Secretary in the same manner and to the same extent as if the plan were not in effect, and

(8) provides that the State agency will make such reports to the Secretary in such form and containing such information, as the Secretary shall from time to time require.

(d) If the Secretary rejects a plan submitted under subsection (b), he shall afford the State submitting the plan due notice and opportunity for a hearing before so doing.

(e) After the Secretary approves a State plan submitted under subsection (b), he may, but shall not be required to, exercise his authority under sections 8, 9, 10, 13, and 17 with respect to comparable standards promulgated under section 6, for the period specified in the next sentence. The Secretary may exercise the authority referred to above until he determines, on the basis of actual operations under the State plan, that the criteria set forth in subsection (c) are being applied, but he shall not make such determination for at least three years after the plan's approval under subsection (c). Upon making the determination referred to in the preceding sen tence, the provisions of sections 5(a)(2), 8 (except for the purpose of carrying out subsection (f) of this section), 9, 10, 13, and 17, and standards promulgated under section 6 of this Act, shall not apply with respect to any occupational safety or health issues covered under the plan, but the Secretary may retain jurisdiction under the above provisions in any proceeding commenced under section 9 or 10 before the date of determination.

(f) The Secretary shall, on the basis of reports submitted by the State agency and his own inspections make a continuing evaluation of the manner in which each State having a plan approved under this section is carrying out such plan. Whenever the Secretary finds, after affording due notice and opportunity for a hearing, that in the administration of the State plan there is a failure to comply sub stantially with any provision of the State plan (or any assurance contained therein), he shall notify the State agency of his withdrawal of approval of such plan and upon receipt of such notice such plan shall cease to be in effect, but the State may retain jurisdiction in any case commenced before the withdrawal of the plan in order to enforce standards under the plan whenever the issues involved do not relate to the reasons for the withdrawal of the plan.

(g) The State may obtain a review of a decision of the Secretary withdrawing approval of or rejecting its plan by the United States court of appeals for the circuit

29 USC 667

in which the State is located by filing in such court within thirty days following receipt of notice of such decision a petition to modify or set aside in whole or in part the action of the Secretary. A copy of such petition shall forthwith be served upon the Secretary, and thereupon the Secretary shall certify and file in the court the record upon which the decision complained of was issued as provided in sec tion 2112 of title 28, United States Code. Unless the court finds that the Secretary's decision in rejecting a proposed State plan or withdrawing his approval of such a plan is not supported by substantial evidence the court shall affirm the Secretary's decision. The judgment of the court shall be subject to review by the Supreme Court of the United States upon certiorari or certification as provided in section 1254 of title 28, United States Code.

(h) The Secretary may enter into an agreement with a State under which the State will be permitted to continue to enforce one or more occupational health and safety standards in effect in such State until final action is taken by the Secretary with respect to a plan submitted by a State under subsection (b) of this section, or two years from the date of enactment of this Act, whichever is earlier.

SEC. 19. FEDERAL AGENCY SAFETY PROGRAMS AND RESPONSIBILITIES

(a) It shall be the responsibility of the head of each Federal agency (not includ ing the United States Postal Service) to establish and maintain an effective and comprehensive occupational safety and health program which is consistent with the standards promulgated under section 6. The head of each agency shall (after consultation with representatives of the employees thereof)

29 USC 668

Pub. L. 150-241

(1) provide safe and healthful places and conditions of employment, con sistent with the standards set under section 6;

(2) acquire, maintain, and require the use of safety equipment, personal protective equipment, and devices reasonably necessary to protect employees;

(3) keep adequate records of all occupational accidents and illnesses for proper evaluation and necessary corrective action;

(4) consult with the Secretary with regard to the adequacy as to form and content of records kept pursuant to subsection (a)(3) of this section; and

(5) make an annual report to the Secretary with respect to occupational accidents and injuries and the agency's program under this section. Such report shall include any report submitted under section 7902(e)(2) of title 5, United States Code.

(b) The Secretary shall report to the President a summary or digest of reports submitted to him under subsection (a)(5) of this section, together with his evalua tions of and recommendations derived from such reports.

Pub. L. 97-375

(c) Section 7902(c)(1) of title 5, United States Code, is amended by inserting after "agencies" the following: "and of labor organizations representing employ ees".

(d) The Secretary shall have access to records and reports kept and filed by Federal agencies pursuant to subsections (a)(3) and (5) of this section unless those records and reports are specifically required by Executive order to be kept secret in the interest of the national defense or foreign policy, in which case the Secretary shall have access to such information as will not jeopardize national defense or for eign policy.

29 USC 669

SEC. 20. RESEARCH AND RELATED ACTIVITIES

29 USC 669

(a) (1) The Secretary of Health and Human Services, after consultation with the Secretary and with other appropriate Federal departments or agencies, shall conduct (directly or by grants or contracts) research, experiments, and demon strations relating to occupational safety and health, including studies of psy chological factors involved, and relating to innovative methods, techniques, and approaches for dealing with occupational safety and health problems.

(2) The Secretary of Health and Human Services shall from time to time consult with the Secretary in order to develop specific plans for such research, demonstrations, and experiments as are necessary to produce criteria, includ ing criteria identifying toxic substances, enabling the Secretary to meet his responsibility for the formulation of safety and health standards under this Act; and the Secretary of Health and Human Services, on the basis of such research, demonstrations, and experiments and any other information available to him, shall develop and publish at least annually such criteria as will effectuate the purposes of this Act.

(3) The Secretary of Health and Human Services, on the basis of such research, demonstrations, and experiments, and any other information avail able to him, shall develop criteria dealing with toxic materials and harmful physical agents and substances which will describe exposure levels that are safe for various periods of employment, including but not limited to the expo sure levels at which no employee will suffer impaired health or functional capacities or diminished life expectancy as a result of his work experience.

(4) The Secretary of Health and Human Services shall also conduct special research, experiments, and demonstrations relating to occupational safety and health as are necessary to explore new problems, including those created by new technology in occupational safety and health, which may require amelio rative action beyond that which is otherwise provided for in the operating pro visions of this Act. The Secretary of Health and Human Services shall also con duct research into the motivational and behavioral factors relating to the field of occupational safety and health.

(5) The Secretary of Health and Human Services, in order to comply with his responsibilities under paragraph (2), and in order to develop needed infor mation regarding potentially toxic substances or harmful physical agents, may prescribe regulations requiring employers to measure, record, and make reports on the exposure of employees to substances or physical agents which the Secretary of Health and Human Services reasonably believes may endanger the health or safety of employees. The Secretary of Health and Human Services also is authorized to establish such programs of medical examinations and tests as may be necessary for determining the incidence of occupational illnesses and the susceptibility of employees to such illnesses. Nothing in this or any other provision of this Act shall be deemed to authorize or require medical examination, immunization, or treatment for those who object thereto on reli gious grounds, except where such is necessary for the protection of the health or safety of others. Upon the request of any employer who is required to meas ure and record exposure of employees to substances or physical agents as pro vided under this subsection, the Secretary of Health and Human Services shall furnish full financial or other assistance to such employer for the purpose of defraying any additional expense incurred by him in carrying out the measur ing and recording as provided in this subsection.

(6) The Secretary of Health and Human Services shall publish within six months of enactment of this Act and thereafter as needed but at least annually a list of all known toxic substances by generic family or other useful grouping, and the concentrations at which such toxicity is known to occur. He shall deter

29 USC 669

mine following a written request by any employer or authorized representative of employees, specifying with reasonable particularity the grounds on which the request is made, whether any substance normally found in the place of employment has potentially toxic effects in such concentrations as used or found; and shall submit such determination both to employers and affected employees as soon as possible. If the Secretary of Health and Human Services determines that any substance is potentially toxic at the concentrations in which it is used or found in a place of employment, and such substance is not covered by an occupational safety or health standard promulgated under sec tion 6, the Secretary of Health and Human Services shall immediately submit such determination to the Secretary, together with all pertinent criteria.

(7) Within two years of enactment of the Act, and annually thereafter the Secretary of Health and Human Services shall conduct and publish industry wide studies of the effect of chronic or low level exposure to industrial mate rials, processes, and stresses on the potential for illness, disease, or loss of func tional capacity in aging adults.

(b) The Secretary of Health and Human Services is authorized to make inspec tions and question employers and employees as provided in section 8 of this Act in order to carry out his functions and responsibilities under this section.

(c) The Secretary is authorized to enter into contracts, agreements, or other arrangements with appropriate public agencies or private organizations for the pur pose of conducting studies relating to his responsibilities under this Act. In carry ing out his responsibilities under this subsection, the Secretary shall cooperate with the Secretary of Health and Human Services in order to avoid any duplication of efforts under this section.

(d) Information obtained by the Secretary and the Secretary of Health and Human Services under this section shall be disseminated by the Secretary to employers and employees and organizations thereof.

(e) The functions of the Secretary of Health and Human Services under this Act shall, to the extent feasible, be delegated to the Director of the National Institute for Occupational Safety and Health established by section 22 of this Act.

EXPANDED RESEARCH ON WORKER SAFETY AND HEALTH

The Secretary of Health and Human Services (referred to in this section as the "Secretary"), acting through the Director of the National Institute of Occupational Safety and Health, shall enhance and expand research as deemed appropriate on the health and safety of workers who are at risk for bioterrorist threats or attacks in the workplace, including research on the health effects of measures taken to treat or protect such workers for diseases or disorders resulting from a bioterrorist threat or attack. Nothing in this section may be construed as establishing new regulatory authority for the Secretary or the Director to issue or modify any occupational safe ty and health rule or regulation.

29 USC 669a

Pub. L. 107-188, Title I, § 153 added this text.

SEC. 21. TRAINING AND EMPLOYEE EDUCATION

(a) The Secretary of Health and Human Services, after consultation with the Secretary and with other appropriate Federal departments and agencies, shall con duct, directly or by grants or contracts

(1) education programs to provide an adequate supply of qualified person nel to carry out the purposes of this Act, and

(2) informational programs on the importance of and proper use of ade quate safety and health equipment.

(b) The Secretary is also authorized to conduct, directly or by grants or con tracts, short term training of personnel engaged in work related to his responsibil ities under this Act.

29 USC 670

Pub. L. 96-88 substituted Secretary of Health and Human Services for Secretary of Health, Education, and Welfare.

29 USC 670

(c) The Secretary, in consultation with the Secretary of Health and Human Services, shall

(1) provide for the establishment and supervision of programs for the education and training of employers and employees in the recognition, avoidance, and prevention of unsafe or unhealthful working conditions in employments covered by this Act, and

Pub. L. 105-97, §2 added subsection (d). *See Historical notes.*

(2) consult with and advise employers and employees, and organizations representing employers and employees as to effective means of preventing occupational injuries and illnesses.

(d) (1) The Secretary shall establish and support cooperative agreements with the States under which employers subject to this Act may consult with State personnel with respect to

(A) the application of occupational safety and health requirements under this Act or under State plans approved under section 18; and

(B) voluntary efforts that employers may undertake to establish and maintain safe and healthful employment and places of employment. Such agreements may provide, as a condition of receiving funds under such agreements, for contributions by States towards meeting the costs of such agreements.

(2) Pursuant to such agreements the State shall provide on site consultation at the employer's worksite to employers who request such assistance. The State may also provide other education and training programs for employers and employees in the State. The State shall ensure that on site consultations conducted pursuant to such agreements include provision for the participation by employees.

(3) Activities under this subsection shall be conducted independently of any enforcement activity. If an employer fails to take immediate action to eliminate employee exposure to an imminent danger identified in a consultation or fails to correct a serious hazard so identified within a reasonable time, a report shall be made to the appropriate enforcement authority for such action as is appropriate.

(4) The Secretary shall, by regulation after notice and opportunity for comment, establish rules under which an employer

(A) which requests and undergoes an on site consultative visit provided under this subsection;

(B) which corrects the hazards that have been identified during the visit within the time frames established by the State and agrees to request a subsequent consultative visit if major changes in working conditions or work processes occur which introduce new hazards in the workplace; and

(C) which is implementing procedures for regularly identifying and preventing hazards regulated under this Act and maintains appropriate involvement of, and training for, management and non management employees in achieving safe and healthful working conditions,

may be exempt from an inspection (except an inspection requested under section 8(f) or an inspection to determine the cause of a workplace accident which resulted in the death of one or more employees or hospitalization for three or more employees) for a period of 1 year from the closing of the consultative visit.

(5) A State shall provide worksite consultations under paragraph (2) at the request of an employer. Priority in scheduling such consultations shall be assigned to requests from small businesses which are in higher hazard industries or have the most hazardous conditions at issue in the request.

SEC. 22. NATIONAL INSTITUTE FOR OCCUPATIONAL SAFETY AND HEALTH

29 USC 671

(a) It is the purpose of this section to establish a National Institute for Occupational Safety and Health in the Department of Health and Human Services in order to carry out the policy set forth in section 2 of this Act and to perform the

29 USC 671

functions of the Secretary of Health and Human Services under sections 20 and 21 of this Act.

(b) There is hereby established in the Department of Health and Human Services a National Institute for Occupational Safety and Health. The Institute shall be headed by a Director who shall be appointed by the Secretary of Health and Human Services, and who shall serve for a term of six years unless previously removed by the Secretary of Health and Human Services.

(c) The Institute is authorized to

(1) develop and establish recommended occupational safety and health standards; and

(2) perform all functions of the Secretary of Health and Human Services under sections 20 and 21 of this Act.

(d) Upon his own initiative, or upon the request of the Secretary of Health and Human Services, the Director is authorized (1) to conduct such research and experimental programs as he determines are necessary for the development of criteria for new and improved occupational safety and health standards, and (2) after consideration of the results of such research and experimental programs make recommendations concerning new or improved occupational safety and health standards. Any occupational safety and health standard recommended pursuant to this section shall immediately be forwarded to the Secretary of Labor, and to the Secretary of Health and Human Services.

(e) In addition to any authority vested in the Institute by other provisions of this section, the Director, in carrying out the functions of the Institute, is authorized to

(1) prescribe such regulations as he deems necessary governing the manner in which its functions shall be carried out;

(2) receive money and other property donated, bequeathed, or devised, without condition or restriction other than that it be used for the purposes of the Institute and to use, sell, or otherwise dispose of such property for the purpose of carrying out its functions;

(3) receive (and use, sell, or otherwise dispose of, in accordance with paragraph (2)), money and other property donated, bequeathed, or devised to the Institute with a condition or restriction, including a condition that the Institute use other funds of the Institute for the purposes of the gift;

(4) in accordance with the civil service laws, appoint and fix the compensation of such personnel as may be necessary to carry out the provisions of this section;

(5) obtain the services of experts and consultants in accordance with the provisions of section 3109 of title 5, United States Code;

(6) accept and utilize the services of voluntary and noncompensated personnel and reimburse them for travel expenses, including per diem, as authorized by section 5703 of title 5, United States Code;

(7) enter into contracts, grants or other arrangements, or modifications thereof to carry out the provisions of this section, and such contracts or modifications thereof may be entered into without performance or other bonds, and without regard to section 3709 of the Revised Statutes, as amended (41 U.S.C. 5), or any other provision of law relating to competitive bidding;

(8) make advance, progress, and other payments which the Director deems necessary under this title without regard to the provisions of section 3324 (a) and (b) of Title 31; and

Pub. L. 97-258

(9) make other necessary expenditures.

(f) The Director shall submit to the Secretary of Health and Human Services, to the President, and to the Congress an annual report of the operations of the Institute under this Act, which shall include a detailed statement of all private and public funds received and expended by it, and such recommendations as he deems appropriate.

(g) Lead Based Paint Activities.

Pub. L. 102-550
added subsection (g).

29 USC 671

(1) Training Grant Program.

(A) The Institute, in conjunction with the Administrator of the Environmental Protection Agency, may make grants for the training and education of workers and supervisors who are or may be directly engaged in lead based paint activities.

(B) Grants referred to in subparagraph (A) shall be awarded to nonprofit organizations (including colleges and universities, joint labor management trust funds, States, and nonprofit government employee organizations)

15 USC 2681 et. seq.

(i) which are engaged in the training and education of workers and supervisors who are or who may be directly engaged in lead based paint activities (as defined in Title IV of the Toxic Substances Control Act),

(ii) which have demonstrated experience in implementing and operating health and safety training and education programs, and

(iii) with a demonstrated ability to reach, and involve in lead based paint training programs, target populations of individuals who are or will be engaged in lead based paint activities.

Grants under this subsection shall be awarded only to those organizations that fund at least 30 percent of their lead based paint activities training programs from non Federal sources, excluding in kind contributions. Grants may also be made to local governments to carry out such training and education for their employees.

(C) There are authorized to be appropriated, a minimum, $10,000,000 to the Institute for each of the fiscal years 1994 through 1997 to make grants under this paragraph.

(2) Evaluation of Programs. The Institute shall conduct periodic and comprehensive assessments of the efficacy of the worker and supervisor training programs developed and offered by those receiving grants under this section. The Director shall prepare reports on the results of these assessments addressed to the Administrator of the Environmental Protection Agency to include recommendations as may be appropriate for the revision of these programs. The sum of $500,000 is authorized to be appropriated to the Institute for each of the fiscal years 1994 through 1997 to carry out this paragraph.

WORKERS' FAMILY PROTECTION

29 USC 671a

(a) Short title

This section may be cited as the ``Workers' Family Protection Act''.

Pub. L. 102-522, Title II, §209 added this text.

(b) Findings and purpose

(1) Findings

Congress finds that

(A) hazardous chemicals and substances that can threaten the health and safety of workers are being transported out of industries on workers' clothing and persons;

(B) these chemicals and substances have the potential to pose an additional threat to the health and welfare of workers and their families;

(C) additional information is needed concerning issues related to employee transported contaminant releases; and

(D) additional regulations may be needed to prevent future releases of this type.

(2) Purpose

It is the purpose of this section to

(A) increase understanding and awareness concerning the extent and possible health impacts of the problems and incidents described in paragraph (1);

(B) prevent or mitigate future incidents of home contamination that could adversely affect the health and safety of workers and their families;

(C) clarify regulatory authority for preventing and responding to such incidents; and

(D) assist workers in redressing and responding to such incidents when they occur.

(c) Evaluation of employee transported contaminant releases

(1) Study

(A) In general

Not later than 18 months after October 26, 1992, the Director of the National Institute for Occupational Safety and Health (hereafter in this sec tion referred to as the "Director"), in cooperation with the Secretary of Labor, the Administrator of the Environmental Protection Agency, the Administrator of the Agency for Toxic Substances and Disease Registry, and the heads of other Federal Government agencies as determined to be appro priate by the Director, shall conduct a study to evaluate the potential for, the prevalence of, and the issues related to the contamination of workers' homes with hazardous chemicals and substances, including infectious agents, trans ported from the workplaces of such workers.

(B) Matters to be evaluated

In conducting the study and evaluation under subparagraph (A), the Director shall

(i) conduct a review of past incidents of home contamination through the utilization of literature and of records concerning past investigations and enforcement actions undertaken by

(I) the National Institute for Occupational Safety and Health;

(II) the Secretary of Labor to enforce the Occupational Safety and Health Act of 1970 (29 U.S.C. 651 et seq.);

(III) States to enforce occupational safety and health standards in accordance with section 18 of such Act (29 U.S.C. 667); and

(IV) other government agencies (including the Department of Energy and the Environmental Protection Agency), as the Director may determine to be appropriate;

(ii) evaluate current statutory, regulatory, and voluntary industrial hygiene or other measures used by small, medium and large employers to prevent or remediate home contamination;

(iii) compile a summary of the existing research and case histories conducted on incidents of employee transported contaminant releases, including

(I) the effectiveness of workplace housekeeping practices and personal protective equipment in preventing such incidents;

(II) the health effects, if any, of the resulting exposure on work ers and their families;

(III) the effectiveness of normal house cleaning and laundry pro cedures for removing hazardous materials and agents from workers' homes and personal clothing;

(IV) indoor air quality, as the research concerning such pertains to the fate of chemicals transported from a workplace into the home environment; and

(V) methods for differentiating exposure health effects and rela tive risks associated with specific agents from other sources of expo sure inside and outside the home;

(iv) identify the role of Federal and State agencies in responding to incidents of home contamination;

(v) prepare and submit to the Task Force established under paragraph (2) and to the appropriate committees of Congress, a report concerning the results of the matters studied or evaluated under clauses (i) through (iv); and

(vi) study home contamination incidents and issues and worker and family protection policies and practices related to the special circum stances of firefighters and prepare and submit to the appropriate com mittees of Congress a report concerning the findings with respect to such study.

(2) Development of investigative strategy

(A) Task Force

Not later than 12 months after October 26, 1992, the Director shall estab lish a working group, to be known as the "Workers' Family Protection Task Force". The Task Force shall

(i) be composed of not more than 15 individuals to be appointed by the Director from among individuals who are representative of workers, industry, scientists, industrial hygienists, the National Research Council, and government agencies, except that not more than one such individual shall be from each appropriate government agency and the number of individuals appointed to represent industry and workers shall be equal in number;

(ii) review the report submitted under paragraph (1)(B)(v);

(iii) determine, with respect to such report, the additional data needs, if any, and the need for additional evaluation of the scientific issues relat ed to and the feasibility of developing such additional data; and

(iv) if additional data are determined by the Task Force to be need ed, develop a recommended investigative strategy for use in obtaining such information.

(B) Investigative strategy

(i) Content

The investigative strategy developed under subparagraph (A)(iv) shall identify data gaps that can and cannot be filled, assumptions and uncertainties associated with various components of such strategy, a timetable for the implementation of such strategy, and methodologies used to gather any required data.

(ii) Peer review

The Director shall publish the proposed investigative strategy under subparagraph (A)(iv) for public comment and utilize other methods, including technical conferences or seminars, for the purpose of obtain ing comments concerning the proposed strategy.

(iii) Final strategy

After the peer review and public comment is conducted under clause (ii), the Director, in consultation with the heads of other government agencies, shall propose a final strategy for investigating issues related to home contamination that shall be implemented by the National Institute for Occupational Safety and Health and other Federal agencies for the period of time necessary to enable such agencies to obtain the informa tion identified under subparagraph (A)(iii).

(C) Construction

Nothing in this section shall be construed as precluding any government agency from investigating issues related to home contamination using exist ing procedures until such time as a final strategy is developed or from tak ing actions in addition to those proposed in the strategy after its completion.

(3) Implementation of investigative strategy

Upon completion of the investigative strategy under subparagraph (B)(iii), each Federal agency or department shall fulfill the role assigned to it by the strategy.

29 USC 671a

(d) Regulations

(1) In general

Not later than 4 years after October 26, 1992, and periodically thereafter, the Secretary of Labor, based on the information developed under subsection (c) of this section and on other information available to the Secretary, shall

(A) determine if additional education about, emphasis on, or enforce ment of existing regulations or standards is needed and will be sufficient, or if additional regulations or standards are needed with regard to employee transported releases of hazardous materials; and

(B) prepare and submit to the appropriate committees of Congress a report concerning the result of such determination.

(2) Additional regulations or standards

If the Secretary of Labor determines that additional regulations or stan dards are needed under paragraph (1), the Secretary shall promulgate, pursuant to the Secretary's authority under the Occupational Safety and Health Act of 1970 (29 U.S.C. 651 et seq.), such regulations or standards as determined to be appropriate not later than 3 years after such determination.

(e) Authorization of appropriations

There are authorized to be appropriated from sums otherwise authorized to be appropriated, for each fiscal year such sums as may be necessary to carry out this section.

SEC. 23. GRANTS TO THE STATES

(a) The Secretary is authorized, during the fiscal year ending June 30, 1971,   29 USC 672
and the two succeeding fiscal years, to make grants to the States which have des ignated a State agency under section 18 to assist them

(1) in identifying their needs and responsibilities in the area of occupation al safety and health,

(2) in developing State plans under section 18, or

(3) in developing plans for

(A) establishing systems for the collection of information concerning the nature and frequency of occupational injuries and diseases;

(B) increasing the expertise and enforcement capabilities of their per sonnel engaged in occupational safety and health programs; or

(C) otherwise improving the administration and enforcement of State occupational safety and health laws, including standards thereunder, consis tent with the objectives of this Act.

(b) The Secretary is authorized, during the fiscal year ending June 30, 1971, and the two succeeding fiscal years, to make grants to the States for experimental and demonstration projects consistent with the objectives set forth in subsection (a) of this section.

(c) The Governor of the State shall designate the appropriate State agency for receipt of any grant made by the Secretary under this section.

(d) Any State agency designated by the Governor of the State desiring a grant under this section shall submit an application therefor to the Secretary.

(e) The Secretary shall review the application, and shall, after consultation with the Secretary of Health and Human Services, approve or reject such application.

(f) The Federal share for each State grant under subsection (a) or (b) of this sec tion may not exceed 90 per centum of the total cost of the application. In the event the Federal share for all States under either such subsection is not the same, the dif ferences among the States shall be established on the basis of objective criteria.

(g) The Secretary is authorized to make grants to the States to assist them in administering and enforcing programs for occupational safety and health contained

29 USC 672

in State plans approved by the Secretary pursuant to section 18 of this Act. The Federal share for each State grant under this subsection may not exceed 50 per cen tum of the total cost to the State of such a program. The last sentence of subsection (f) shall be applicable in determining the Federal share under this subsection.

(h) Prior to June 30, 1973, the Secretary shall, after consultation with the Secretary of Health and Human Services, transmit a report to the President and to the Congress, describing the experience under the grant programs authorized by this section and making any recommendations he may deem appropriate.

SEC. 24. STATISTICS

29 USC 673

(a) In order to further the purposes of this Act, the Secretary, in consultation with the Secretary of Health and Human Services, shall develop and maintain an effective program of collection, compilation, and analysis of occupational safety and health statistics. Such program may cover all employments whether or not sub ject to any other provisions of this Act but shall not cover employments excluded by section 4 of the Act. The Secretary shall compile accurate statistics on work injuries and illnesses which shall include all disabling, serious, or significant injuries and illnesses, whether or not involving loss of time from work, other than minor injuries requiring only first aid treatment and which do not involve medical treatment, loss of consciousness, restriction of work or motion, or transfer to anoth er job.

(b) To carry out his duties under subsection (a) of this section, the Secretary may

(1) promote, encourage, or directly engage in programs of studies, informa tion and communication concerning occupational safety and health statistics;

(2) make grants to States or political subdivisions thereof in order to assist them in developing and administering programs dealing with occupational safety and health statistics; and

(3) arrange, through grants or contracts, for the conduct of such research and investigations as give promise of furthering the objectives of this section.

(c) The Federal share for each grant under subsection (b) of this section may be up to 50 per centum of the State's total cost.

(d) The Secretary may, with the consent of any State or political subdivision thereof, accept and use the services, facilities, and employees of the agencies of such State or political subdivision, with or without reimbursement, in order to assist him in carrying out his functions under this section.

(e) On the basis of the records made and kept pursuant to section 8(c) of this Act, employers shall file such reports with the Secretary as he shall prescribe by regulation, as necessary to carry out his functions under this Act.

(f) Agreements between the Department of Labor and States pertaining to the collection of occupational safety and health statistics already in effect on the effec tive date of this Act shall remain in effect until superseded by grants or contracts made under this Act.

SEC. 25. AUDITS

29 USC 674

(a) Each recipient of a grant under this Act shall keep such records as the Secretary or the Secretary of Health and Human Services shall prescribe, includ ing records which fully disclose the amount and disposition by such recipient of the proceeds of such grant, the total cost of the project or undertaking in connec tion with which such grant is made or used, and the amount of that portion of the cost of the project or undertaking supplied by other sources, and such other records as will facilitate an effective audit.

29 USC 674

(b) The Secretary or the Secretary of Health and Human Services, and the Comptroller General of the United States, or any of their duly authorized repre sentatives, shall have access for the purpose of audit and examination to any books, documents, papers, and records of the recipients of any grant under this Act that are pertinent to any such grant.

SEC. 26. ANNUAL REPORT

Within one hundred and twenty days following the convening of each regular session of each Congress, the Secretary and the Secretary of Health and Human Services shall each prepare and submit to the President for transmittal to the Congress a report upon the subject matter of this Act, the progress toward achievement of the purpose of this Act, the needs and requirements in the field of occupational safety and health, and any other relevant information. Such reports shall include information regarding occupational safety and health standards, and criteria for such standards, developed during the preceding year; evaluation of stan dards and criteria previously developed under this Act, defining areas of emphasis for new criteria and standards; an evaluation of the degree of observance of appli cable occupational safety and health standards, and a summary of inspection and enforcement activity undertaken; analysis and evaluation of research activities for which results have been obtained under governmental and nongovernmental spon sorship; an analysis of major occupational diseases; evaluation of available control and measurement technology for hazards for which standards or criteria have been developed during the preceding year; description of cooperative efforts undertak en between Government agencies and other interested parties in the implementa tion of this Act during the preceding year; a progress report on the development of an adequate supply of trained manpower in the field of occupational safety and health, including estimates of future needs and the efforts being made by Government and others to meet those needs; listing of all toxic substances in indus trial usage for which labeling requirements, criteria, or standards have not yet been established; and such recommendations for additional legislation as are deemed necessary to protect the safety and health of the worker and improve the adminis tration of this Act.

29 USC 675

Pub. L. 104-66 §3003 terminated provision relating to transmittal of report to Congress.

SEC. 27. NATIONAL COMMISSION ON STATE WORKMEN'S COMPENSATION LAWS

29 USC 676

(Text omitted.)

See notes on omitted text.

SEC. 28. ECONOMIC ASSISTANCE TO SMALL BUSINESSES

(Text omitted.)

See notes on omitted text.

SEC. 29. ADDITIONAL ASSISTANT SECRETARY OF LABOR

(Text omitted.)

See notes on omitted text.

SEC. 30. ADDITIONAL POSITIONS

(Text omitted.)

See notes on omitted text.

SEC. 31. EMERGENCY LOCATOR BEACONS

(Text omitted.)

See notes on omitted text.

29 USC 677

SEC. 32. SEPARABILITY

29 USC 677   If any provision of this Act, or the application of such provision to any person or circumstance, shall be held invalid, the remainder of this Act, or the application of such provision to persons or circumstances other than those as to which it is held invalid, shall not be affected thereby.

SEC. 33. APPROPRIATIONS

29 USC 678   There are authorized to be appropriated to carry out this Act for each fiscal year such sums as the Congress shall deem necessary.

SEC. 34. EFFECTIVE DATE

This Act shall take effect one hundred and twenty days after the date of its enact ment.

Approved December 29, 1970.
As amended through January 1, 2004.

HISTORICAL NOTES

This reprint generally retains the section numbers originally created by Congress in the Occupational Safety and Health (OSH) Act of 1970, Pub. L. 91 596, 84 Stat. 1590. This document includes some editorial changes, such as changing the for mat to make it easier to read, correcting typographical errors, and updating some of the margin notes. Because Congress enacted amendments to the Act since 1970, this version differs from the original version of the OSH Act. It also differs slight ly from the version published in the United States Code at 29 U.S.C. 661 *et seq*. For example, this reprint refers to the statute as the "Act" rather than the "chapter."

This reprint reflects the provisions of the OSH Act that are in effect as of January 1, 2004. Citations to Public Laws which made important amendments to the OSH Act since 1970 are set forth in the margins and explanatory notes are included below.

NOTE: Some provisions of the OSH Act may be affected by the enactment of, or amendments to, other statutes. Section 17(h)(1), 29 U.S.C. 666, is an example. The original provision amended section 1114 of title 18 of the United States Code to include employees of "the Department of Labor assigned to perform investiga tive, inspection, or law enforcement functions" within the list of persons protected by the provisions to allow prosecution of persons who have killed or attempted to kill an officer or employee of the U.S. government while performing official duties. This reprint sets forth the text of section 17(h) as enacted in 1970. However, since 1970, Congress has enacted multiple amendments to 18 U.S.C. 1114. The current version does not specifically include the Department of Labor in a list; rather it states that "Whoever kills or attempts to kill any officer or employee of the United States or of any agency in any branch of the United States Government (including any member of the uniformed services) while such officer or employee is engaged in or on account of the performance of official duties, or any person assisting such an officer or employee in the performance of such duties or on account of that assistance shall be punished . . ." as provided by the statute. Readers are reminded that the official version of statutes can be found in the cur rent volumes of the United States Code, and more extensive historical notes can be found in the current volumes of the United States Code Annotated.

Amendments

On January 2, 1974, section 2(c) of Pub. L. 93 237 replaced the phrase "7(b)(6)" in section 28(d) of the OSH Act with "7(b)(5)". 87 Stat. 1023. Note: The text of Section 28 (Economic Assistance to Small Business) amended Sections 7(b) and Section 4(c)(1) of the Small Business Act. Because these amendments are no longer current, the text of section 28 is omitted in this reprint. For the current ver sion, see 15 U.S.C. 636.

In 1977, the U.S. entered into the Panama Canal Treaty of 1977, Sept. 7, 1977, U.S. Panama, T.I.A.S. 10030, 33 U.S.T. 39. In 1979, Congress enacted imple menting legislation. Panama Canal Act of 1979, Pub. L. 96 70, 93 Stat. 452 (1979). Although no corresponding amendment to the OSH Act was enacted, the Canal Zone ceased to exist in 1979. The U.S. continued to manage, operate and facilitate the transit of ships through the Canal under the authority of the Panama Canal Treaty until December 31, 1999, at which time authority over the Canal was trans ferred to the Republic of Panama.

On March 27, 1978, Pub. L. 95 251, 92 Stat. 183, replaced the term "hearing examiner(s)" with "administrative law judge(s)" in all federal laws, including sec tions 12(e), 12(j), and 12(k) of the OSH Act, 29 U.S.C. 661.

On October 13, 1978, Pub. L. 95 454, 92 Stat. 1111, 1221, which redesignated sec tion numbers concerning personnel matters and compensation, resulted in the sub stitution of section 5372 of Title 5 for section 5362 in section 12(e) of the OSH Act, 29 U.S.C. 661.

On October 17, 1979, Pub. L. 96 88, Title V, section 509(b), 93 Stat. 668, 695, redesignated references to the Department of Health, Education, and Welfare to the Department of Health and Human Services and redesignated references to the Secretary of Health, Education, and Welfare to the Secretary of Health and Human Services.

On September 13, 1982, Pub. L. 97 258, §4(b), 96 Stat. 877, 1067, effectively sub stituted "Section 3324(a) and (b) of Title 31" for "Section 3648 of the Revised Statutes, as amended (31 U.S.C. 529)" in section 22 (e)(8), 29 U.S.C. 671, relating to NIOSH procurement authority.

On December 21, 1982, Pub. L. 97 375, 96 Stat. 1819, deleted the sentence in sec tion 19(b) of the Act, 29 U.S.C. 668, that directed the President of the United States to transmit annual reports of the activities of federal agencies to the House of Representatives and the Senate.

On October 12, 1984, Pub. L. 98 473, Chapter II, 98 Stat. 1837, 1987, (common ly referred to as the "Sentencing Reform Act of 1984") instituted a classification system for criminal offenses punishable under the United States Code. Under this system, an offense with imprisonment terms of "six months or less but more than thirty days," such as that found in 29 U.S.C. 666(e) for a willful violation of the OSH Act, is classified as a criminal "Class B misdemeanor." 18 U.S.C. 3559(a)(7). The criminal code increases the monetary penalties for criminal misdemeanors beyond what is provided for in the OSH Act: a fine for a Class B misdemeanor resulting in death, for example, is not more than $250,000 for an individual, and is not more than $500,000 for an organization. 18 U.S.C. 3571(b)(4), (c)(4). The criminal code also provides for authorized terms of probation for both individuals and organizations. 18 U.S.C. 3551, 3561. The term of imprisonment for individuals is the same as that authorized by the OSH Act. 18 U.S.C. 3581(b)(7).

On November 8, 1984, Pub. L. 98 620, 98 Stat. 3335, deleted the last sentence in section 11(a) of the Act, 29 U.S.C. 660, that required petitions filed under the sub section to be heard expeditiously.

On November 5, 1990, Pub. L. 101 508, 104 Stat. 1388, amended section 17 of the Act, 29 U.S.C. 666, by increasing the penalties in section 17(a) from $10,000 for each violation to "$70,000 for each violation, but not less than $5,000 for each willful violation," and increased the limitation on penalties in sections (b), (c), (d), and (i) from $1,000 to $7,000.

On October 26, 1992, Pub. L. 102 522, 106 Stat. 3410, 3420, added to Title 29, section 671a "Workers' Family Protection" to grant authority to the Director of NIOSH to evaluate, investigate and if necessary, for the Secretary of Labor to reg ulate employee transported releases of hazardous material that result from con tamination on the employee's clothing or person and may adversely affect the health and safety of workers and their families. Note: section 671a was enacted as section 209 of the Fire Administration Authorization Act of 1992, but it is reprinted here because it is codified within the chapter that comprises the OSH Act.

On October 28, 1992, the Housing and Community Development Act of 1992, Pub. L. 102 550, 106 Stat. 3672, 3924, amended section 22 of the Act, 29 U.S.C. 671, by adding subsection (g), which requires NIOSH to institute a training grant program for lead based paint activities.

On July 5, 1994, section 7(b) of Pub. L. 103 272, 108 Stat. 745, repealed section 31 of the OSH Act, "Emergency Locator Beacons." Section 1(e) of the same Public Law, however, enacted a modified version of section 31 of the OSH Act. This pro vision, titled "Emergency Locator Transmitters," is codified at 49 U.S.C. 44712.

On December 21, 1995, Section 3003 of Pub. L. 104 66, 109 Stat. 707, as amend ed, effective May 15, 2000, terminated the provisions relating to the transmittal to Congress of reports under section 26 of the OSH Act. 29 U.S.C. 675.

On July 16, 1998, Pub. L. 105 197, 112 Stat. 638, amended section 21 of the Act, 29 U.S.C. 670, by adding subsection (d), which required the Secretary to establish a compliance assistance program by which employers can consult with state per sonnel regarding the application of and compliance with OSHA standards.

On July 16, 1998, Pub. L. 105 198, 112 Stat. 640, amended section 8 of the Act, 29 U.S.C. 657, by adding subsection (h), which forbids the Secretary to use the results of enforcement activities to evaluate the employees involved in such enforcement or to impose quotas or goals.

On September 29, 1998, Pub. L. 105 241, 112 Stat. 1572, amended sections 3(5) and 19(a) of the Act, 29 U.S.C. 652 and 668, to include the United States Postal Service as an "employer" subject to OSHA enforcement.

On June 12, 2002, Pub. L. 107 188, Title I, Section 153, 116 Stat. 631, Congress enacted 29 U.S.C. 669a, to expand research on the "health and safety of workers who are at risk for bioterrorist threats or attacks in the workplace."

Jurisdictional Note

Although no corresponding amendments to the OSH Act have been made, OSHA no longer exercises jurisdiction over the entity formerly known as the Trust Territory of the Pacific Islands. The Trust Territory, which consisted of the Former Japanese Mandated Islands, was established in 1947 by the Security Council of the United Nations, and administered by the United States. *Trusteeship Agreement for the Former Japanese Mandated Islands,* Apr. 2 July 18, 1947, 61 Stat. 3301, T.I.A.S. 1665, 8 U.N.T.S. 189.

From 1947 to 1994, the people of these islands exercised the right of self determi nation conveyed by the Trusteeship four times, resulting in the division of the Trust Territory into four separate entities. Three entities: the Republic of Palau, the Federated States of Micronesia, and the Republic of the Marshall Islands, became "Freely Associated States," to which U.S. Federal Law does not apply. Since the OSH Act is a generally applicable law that applies to Guam, it applies to the Commonwealth of Northern Mariana Islands, which elected to become a "Flag Territory" of the United States. *See Covenant to Establish a Commonwealth of the Northern Mariana Islands in Political Union with the United States of America,* Article V, section 502(a) as contained in Pub. L. 94 24, 90 Stat. 263 (Mar. 24, 1976)[citations to amendments omitted]; 48 U.S.C. 1801 and note (1976); s*ee also Saipan Stevedore Co., Inc. v. Director, Office of Workers' Compensation Programs,* 133 F.3d 717, 722 (9th Cir. 1998)(Longshore and Harbor Workers' Compensation Act applies to the Commonwealth of Northern Mariana Islands pursuant to section 502(a) of the Covenant because the Act has general application to the states and to Guam). For up to date information on the legal status of these freely associated states and territories, contact the Office of Insular Affairs of the Department of the Interior. (Web address: http://www.doi.gov/oia/)

Omitted Text. Reasons for textual deletions vary. Some deletions may result from amendments to the OSH Act; others to subsequent amendments to other statutes which the original provisions of the OSH Act may have amended in 1970. In some instances, the original provision of the OSH Act was date limited and is no longer operative.

The text of section 12(c), 29 U.S.C. 661, is omitted. Subsection (c) amended sec tions 5314 and 5315 of Title 5, United States Code, to add the positions of Chairman and members of the Occupational Safety and Health Review Commission.

The text of section 27, 29 U.S.C. 676, is omitted. Section 27 listed Congressional findings on workers' compensation and established the National Commission on State Workmen's Compensation Laws, which ceased to exist ninety days after the submission of its final report, which was due no later than July 31, 1972.

The text of section 28 (Economic Assistance to Small Business) amended sections 7(b) and section 4(c)(1) of the Small Business Act to allow for small business loans in order to comply with applicable standards. Because these amendments are no longer current, the text is omitted here. For the current version see 15 U.S.C. 636.

The text of section 29, (Additional Assistant Secretary of Labor), created an Assistant Secretary for Occupational Safety and Health, and section 30 (Additional Positions) created additional positions within the Department of Labor and the Occupational Safety and Health Review Commission in order to carry out the pro visions of the OSH Act. The text of these sections is omitted here because it no longer reflects the current statutory provisions for staffing and pay. For current provisions, see 29 U.S.C. 553 and 5 U.S.C. 5108 (c).

Section 31 of the original OSH Act amended 49 U.S.C. 1421 by inserting a section entitled "Emergency Locator Beacons." The text of that section is omitted in this reprint because Pub. L. 103 272, 108 Stat.745, (July 5, 1994), repealed the text of section 31 and enacted a modified version of the provision, entitled "Emergency Locator Transmitters," which is codified at 49 U.S.C. 44712.

Notes on other legislation affecting the administration of the Occupational Safety and Health Act. Sometimes legislation does not directly amend the OSH Act, but does place requirements on the Secretary of Labor either to act or to refrain from acting under the authority of the OSH Act. Included below are some exam ples of such legislation. Please note that this is not intended to be a comprehensive list.

STANDARDS PROMULGATION.
For example, legislation may require the Secretary to promulgate specific stan dards pursuant to authority under section 6 of the OSH Act, 29 U.S.C. 655. Some examples include the following:

Hazardous Waste Operations. Pub. L. 99 499, Title I, section 126(a) (f), 100 Stat. 1613 (1986), as amended by Pub. L. 100 202, section 101(f), Title II, section 201, 101 Stat. 1329 (1987), required the Secretary of Labor to promulgate standards concerning hazardous waste operations.

Chemical Process Safety Management. Pub. L. 101 549, Title III, section 304, 104 Stat. 2399 (1990), required the Secretary of Labor, in coordination with the Administrator of the Environmental Protection Agency, to promulgate a chemical process safety standard.

Hazardous Materials. Pub. L. 101 615, section 29, 104 Stat. 3244 (1990), required the Secretary of Labor, in consultation with the Secretaries of Transportation and Treasury, to issue specific standards concerning the handling of hazardous materi als.

Bloodborne Pathogens Standard. Pub. L. 102 170, Title I, section 100, 105 Stat. 1107 (1991), required the Secretary of Labor to promulgate a final Bloodborne Pathogens standard.

Lead Standard. The Housing and Community Development Act of 1992, Pub. L. 102 550, Title X, sections 1031 and 1032, 106 Stat. 3672 (1992), required the Secretary of Labor to issue an interim final lead standard.

EXTENSION OF COVERAGE.

Sometimes a statute may make some OSH Act provisions applicable to certain entities that are not subject to those provisions by the terms of the OSH Act. For example, the Congressional Accountability Act of 1995, Pub. L. 104 1, 109 Stat. 3, (1995), extended certain OSH Act coverage, such as the duty to comply with Section 5 of the OSH Act, to the Legislative Branch. Among other provisions, this legislation authorizes the General Counsel of the Office of Compliance within the Legislative Branch to exercise the authority granted to the Secretary of Labor in the OSH Act to inspect places of employment and issue a citation or notice to correct the violation found. This statute does not make all the provisions of the OSH Act applicable to the Legislative Branch. Another example is the Medicare Prescription Drug, Improvement, and Modernization Act of 2003, Title IX, Section 947, Pub. L. 108 173, 117 Stat. 2066 (2003), which requires public hospitals not otherwise subject to the OSH Act to comply with OSHA's Bloodborne Pathogens standard, 29 CFR 1910.1030. This statute provides for the imposition and collec tion of civil money penalties by the Department of Health and Human Services in the event that a hospital fails to comply with OSHA's Bloodborne Pathogens stan dard.

PROGRAM CHANGES ENACTED THROUGH APPROPRIATIONS LEGISLATION.

Sometimes an appropriations statute may allow or restrict certain substantive actions by OSHA or the Secretary of Labor. For example, sometimes an appro priations statute may restrict the use of money appropriated to run the Occupational Safety and Health Administration or the Department of Labor. One example of such a restriction, that has been included in OSHA's appropriation for many years, limits the applicability of OSHA requirements with respect to farming operations that employ ten or fewer workers and do not maintain a temporary labor camp. Another example is a restriction that limits OSHA's authority to conduct certain enforcement activity with respect to employers of ten or fewer employees in low hazard industries. See Consolidated Appropriations Act, 2004, Pub. L. 108 199, Div. E Labor, Health and Human Services, and Education, and Related Agencies Appropriations, 2004, Title I Department of Labor, 118 Stat. 3 (2004). Sometimes an appropriations statute may allow OSHA to retain some money col lected to use for occupational safety and health training or grants. For example, the Consolidated Appropriations Act, 2004, Div. E, Title I, cited above, allows OSHA to retain up to $750,000 of training institute course tuition fees per fiscal year for such uses. For the statutory text of currently applicable appropriations provisions, consult the OSHA appropriations statute for the fiscal year in question.

www.ingramcontent.com/pod-product-compliance
Lightning Source LLC
Chambersburg PA
CBHW071554170526
45166CB00004B/1665